The Constitution of Athens

ARISTOTLE

The Constitution of Athens, Aristotle
Jazzybee Verlag Jürgen Beck
86450 Altenmünster, Loschberg 9
Deutschland

Translator: Thomas J. Dymes

ISBN: 9783849692964

Printed by Createspace, North Charleston, SC, USA

www.jazzybee-verlag.de
www.facebook.com/jazzybeeverlag
admin@jazzybee-verlag.de

CONTENTS

INTRODUCTORY.

The treatise on 'The Constitution of Athens' has been translated by me primarily for such English readers as may feel curiosity about a book which has excited, and is still exciting, so much interest in the learned world.

The recovery of such a book, after its loss for so many centuries, is an event in literature; at the same time its argument, largely concerned as it is with the development of democracy at Athens, provides matter of political and practical, rather than of academic, interest for the English reader of to-day.

I have the pleasure of acknowledging here the courtesy of the Trustees of the British Museum in allowing me to translate from their Text, as edited by Mr. Kenyon, and my great obligations to his labours; they form, unquestionably, a contribution of the highest value, particularly on the subject-matter of the book. It can hardly be expected that, minor corrections excepted, any substantive addition of importance can be made for some time; indeed, not until the 'experts' of Europe have had the opportunity of severally recording their views, both as to the text and its matter.

The gaps and corruptions in the text, however interesting to the critic and emendator, will not long detain the English reader or the student. The hiatuses would seem to be few and generally slight, while some of the corrupt passages open up a wide field for the learned and ingenious. In my translation have taken the text with its difficulties as I found it, reproducing as nearly as I could in English what the Greek, corrupt as it might be, appeared to me to contain. In one or two cases, where the text is obviously corrupt, I have perhaps used a little freedom in my endeavour to extract something like an intelligible meaning. I have had no higher ambitions. There has been no attempt or desire on my part to offer a solution of difficulties which are now being dealt with by more competent hands.

The first forty-one chapters, forming about two-thirds of the work, treat of the Constitution, its development and history. The remainder of the book, consisting of twenty-two chapters, furnishes a detailed account of the Council, with some information about the Assembly, and describes the principal offices of state, the modes of appointment, by lot or vote, and their chief functions, concluding with a short mutilated notice of the constitution of the courts of justice.

T. J. D.

26, Blenheim Crescent, Notting Hill, W. March 26, 1891.

EXPLANATION OF TERMS
FOR THE ENGLISH READER.

Officers, or offices of state, magistrates, magistracies = ἀρχαί (archae), particularly the chief executive offices of government. I do not often use 'magistrate' or 'magistracy,' on account of the limited meaning it has got to have in English. Aristotle commonly uses 'office' instead of 'officer.' Archon (ἄρχων), as will be seen early in the book, is the special designation of the highest officers of state, of whom the senior (Eponymus) gave his name to the year, like the Roman consuls, e.g., 'in the archonship of Eukleides.'

People, popular party or side = δῆμος (demus) implying the possession of political rights, as will often be clear from the context, even when no specific exercise of such rights is referred to.

The masses ='the many' and 'the multitude', including 'the people,' or 'popular party,' and such as are not, or at least may not be, in possession of political rights; a more general term than 'the [x]people,' for which, however, in the original it is sometimes used indifferently.

The Council = Βουλή (Boulé), the great council or deliberative assembly of the state, corresponding roughly to the Roman Senate. Its powers and duties are described chap. xlv. foll.

Assembly = Ἐχχλησία (ekklesia), the great legislative assembly of the people (or citizens), described chap. xliii. foll.; its Presidents = πρυτάνεις (prytanes); presidency, their office and its tenure, chap. xliii.

Chairmen = πρόεδροι (proedri), chosen by the 'presidents' out of their own number, chap. xliv.

Juror = διχαστής (dikast); not a real equivalent, as the dikasts acted as judges as well as jurors, and sat in very much larger bodies than our juries.

Tyrant, tyranny = τύραννος (a lord), τυραννίς: a 'tyrant' in Greek political language means one who has unconstitutionally usurped power in a free state, like Peisistratus. It does not, as with us, imply the abuse of such power; indeed, Peisistratus' rule was often spoken of as 'the Golden Age.' Chap. xvi.

Talent =about £250 (with a purchasing power sufficient to build a trireme, chap. xxii.); divided into 60 minae, each mina containing 100 drachmae, a drachma being worth about a franc, and containing six obols.

2

THE CONSTITUTION OF ATHENS.

CHAP. I.: KYLON.

. . . . swearing by sacred objects according to merit. And the guilt of pollution having been brought home to them, their dead bodies were cast out of their tombs, and their family was banished for ever. On this Epimenides the Cretan purified the city.

CHAP. II.: THE OLIGARCHICAL CONSTITUTION.

After this it came to pass that the upper classes and the people were divided by party-strife for a long period, for the form of government was in all respects oligarchical; indeed, the poor were in a state of bondage to the rich, both themselves, their wives, and their children, and were called Pelatæ (bond-slaves for hire), and Hektemori (paying a sixth of the produce as rent); for at this rate of hire they used to work the lands of the rich. Now, the whole of the land was in the hands of a few, and if the cultivators did not pay their rents, they became subject to bondage, both they and their children, and were bound to their creditors on the security of their persons, up to the time of Solon. For he was the first to come forward as the champion of the people. The hardest and bitterest thing then to the majority was that they had no share in the offices of government; not but what they were dissatisfied with everything else, for in nothing, so to say, had they any share.

CHAP. III.: BEFORE DRACO'S TIME.

Now, the form of the old government before the time of Draco was of this kind. Officers of state were appointed on the basis of merit and wealth, and at first remained in office for life, but afterwards for a period of ten years. And the greatest and earliest of the officers of state were the king, and commander-in-chief, and archon; and earliest of these was the office of king, for this was established at the beginning; next followed that of commander-in-chief, owing to some of the kings proving unwarlike, and it was for this reason that they sent for Ion when the need arose; and last (of the three) was the archonship—for most authorities say it was established in the time of Medon, but some in the time of Acastus; and they adduce as evidence the fact that the nine archons swear to exercise their office just as they did in the time of Acastus — as the Codridæ having retired in the time

3

of his kingship . . . Now, which of the two accounts is correct is of little importance, but there is no doubt of the fact having actually occurred in these times: and that it was the last of these offices that was established, there is further evidence . . . . that the archon administers just like the king and the commander-in-chief, but . . . . for which reason it is only recently that the office has become important, its dignity having been increased by the privileges that have been added to it. Thesmothetæ Endnote 002 were appointed many years afterwards, being elected to their offices from the first for a year, for the purpose of recording the enactments in writing, and preserving them against the trial of such as transgressed the law; for which reason it was the sole office that was not established for more than a year. So far, therefore, these take precedence of others. The nine archons did not all live together, but the king occupied what is now called the Boukolium, near the Prytaneum (in confirmation of which even to this day the marriage of the king's wife with Dionysus takes place here), and the archon resides in the Prytaneum, and the commander-in-chief in the Epilyceum. This was formerly called the Polemarchæum, but from the time that Epilycus, when polemarch, rebuilt and furnished it, it was called Epilyceum: and the Thesmothetæ occupied the Thesmotheteum. But in the time of Solon they all lived together in the Thesmotheteum. And they had power to decide law-suits finally, and not as now merely to hold a preliminary inquiry. Such, then, were the arrangements in respect of the officers of state. The duty of the council of the Areopagitæ was to jealously guard the laws, and it administered most of the affairs of state, and those the most important, both by punishing and fining all offenders with authority; for the election of the archons was on the basis of merit and wealth, and of them the Areopagitæ were composed; this is the reason why it is the only office that continues to be held for life up to the present time.

CHAP. IV.: DRACO'S LAWS.

Now, this is a sketch of the first form of government. And after this, at no long interval, when Aristaechmus was archon, Draco made his laws; and this constitution was as follows. Share in the government was assigned to those who provided themselves with arms; and they chose for the nine archons and the treasurers such as were possessed of property to the value of not less than ten minæ free of all encumbrances, and for the other minor offices such as provided themselves with arms, and for generals and commanders of cavalry such as could show property of not less than a hundred minæ free of all encumbrances, and children born in lawful wedlock above ten years of age; these were to be the presidents of the council and generals and commanders of cavalry . . . up to the time of the audit of their accounts . . . . and receiving from the same rating as the generals and commanders of cavalry. The Council was to consist of four hundred and one, selected by lot from the whole body of citizens; such as were over thirty years of age were to obtain this and the other offices by lot, and the same man was not to hold office twice before all had had their turn; and then appointment was to be made afresh by lot. If any member of the Council, when there was a sitting of the Council or Assembly, was absent from the meeting, he had to pay a fine, the Pentakosiomedimnos (the possessor of land which produced five hundred medimni *Endnote 003* yearly) three drachmæ, the Knight two, and the Zeugitæ (those who possessed a team of oxen) one. And the council of Areopagus was the guardian of the laws, and jealously watched the magistrates to see that they administered their offices according to the laws. And an injured party had the right of bringing his indictment before the council of the Areopagitæ, on showing in contravention of what law he had sustained his injury. (But all this was of no avail, because) the lower classes were bound on the security of their persons, as has been said, and the land was in the hands of a few.

CHAP. V.: CIVIL DISSENSIONS; SOLON.

Such being the constitution in the body politic, and the bulk of the people being in bondage to the few, the people was in a state of opposition to the upper classes. As strife ran high, and the two parties had saced each other for a considerable time, they agreed to choose Solon as mediator and archon, and entrusted the constitution to him after he had composed a poem in elegiac metre, of which the beginning is as follows:

'I ponder, and within my soul lie woes,
As I look on the most honourable land in Ionia;'
for he ever took the lead, fighting and disputing vigorously for each side against the other, and afterwards recommended them both to put an end to the existing strife. Now, in power of speech and reputation Solon ranked among the first, but in property and position among the moderately rich, as is admitted by all, and as he himself bears witness in these verses, where he recommends the rich not to be grasping:

'Do ye, quieting in your bosoms your strong hearts,
Who of many good things have had your fill even to surfeit,
With what is moderate nourish your mighty desire; for neither will
We yield, nor shall you have all else as you wish.'
And in his poems generally he fastens on the rich the blame of these divisions; and it is for this reason, at the beginning of his elegy, he says that he fears the love of money and over-weening pride, attributing to them the enmity that existed.

CHAP. VI.: SOLON; CHARGE AGAINST HIM.

Now, Solon, when he had got to be at the head of affairs, made the people free both for the present and the future, by forbidding loans on the security of the person, and he made laws, and a cancelling of all debts both private and public; this they call Seisachtheia (the disburdening ordinance), as having shaken off their burden. It is in regard to these measures that men try to attack his character. For it happened that when Solon was about to make the Seisachtheia, he announced it first to some of the upper class, and then, as the popular side say, his friends stole a march upon him, while the possessors of property bring the injurious charge that he made a profit himself.

For these friends borrowed money and bought up a great quantity of land, and as the cancelling of debts took place not long afterwards, they became at once rich; this, they say, is the origin of the class who afterwards had the reputation of being rich from of old. Not but what the account of the popular side is the more trustworthy; for it is not reasonable that in all other respects he should have shown himself so moderate and impartial— while it rested entirely with himself whether, or not, he would, by introducing his laws in an underhand way, make himself master of the state, and so an object of hatred to both sides, as also, whether, or not, he would prefer honour and the salvation of the state to any greed for his own gain— it is not reasonable, I say, to suppose that in such petty and unworthy matters he would defile himself. That he possessed such power, and remedied the distempered state of affairs, both he himself records in many passages of his poems, and all others agree. This charge, therefore, should be adjudged false.

CHAP. VII.: HIS CONSTITUTION.

So he established a constitution and made other laws, and they ceased to use the laws of Draco, except in matters of homicide. They inscribed the laws on the tablets, *Endnote 004* and placed them in the court where the king archon sat, and all swore to abide by them; and the nine archons, swearing beside the stone, declared that they would make an offering of a gold statue if they transgressed any of the laws; hence it is that they so swear even to this day. And he ratified the laws for a hundred years, and constituted the government in the following way: He divided property qualifications into four ratings, just as a division had existed before, viz., the Pentakosiomedimnos, the Knight, the Zeugites, and the Thes (poorest class). He assigned as officers of state out of Pentakosiomedimni and Knights and Zeugitæ, the nine archons and the treasurers, and the government-sellers *Endnote 005* and the Eleven and the Kolakratæ, to each class assigning office in proportion to the magnitude of its assessment. To the class of Thetes he gave a share only in the Assembly and courts of justice. And all had to class as Pentakosiomedimni who, from their own property, made five hundred measures, dry and wet combined, and in the class of Knights such as made three hundred, or, as some say, were able to keep a horse: the latter bring as evidence both the name of the class, as if it had been given from that fact, as well as the votive offerings of men of old; for there is an offering in the Acropolis of a figure of Diphilus with the following inscription:

'Anthemion dedicated this figure of Diphilus to the gods
When he exchanged the thetic rating for the knightly rank.'

And there stands beside it a horse, witnessing that it means the class of Knights. Not but what it is more reasonable that they were classified by measures just in the same way as the Pentakosiomedimni. And all had to be rated as Zeugitæ who made two hundred measures combined, and all the rest as Thetes, having no share in any office of state; for which reason even now, if anyone going to be elected to an office were asked in what class he was rated, he would never think of saying in that of the Thetes.

CHAP. VIII.: SOLON'S CONSTITUTION.

He caused the officers of state to be appointed by lot from candidates whom each of the tribes selected. For each selected ten for the nine archons; hence it is that it is still the practice of the tribes for each to appoint ten by lot, and then to appoint by lot from them. And evidence that they caused qualified persons to be appointed by lot is afforded by the law regarding the treasurers, which law they have continued to make use of even to this day, for it ordains that treasurers should be appointed by lot from Pentakosiomedimni. Solon, then, thus legislated regarding the nine archons. For in old days the council on Mars' Hill decided, after citation, on its own authority who was the proper man for each of the offices of state, and invested him accordingly, making the appointment for a year. Now, there were four tribes just as before, and four tribe-kings. Each tribe was divided into three Trittyes (thirds of a tribe) and twelve Naukrariæ. Magistrates of the Naukrariæ were appointed, viz., the Naukrari, who had charge of the current revenues and expenditure; and this is the reason why (as is probable) it is ordained in the laws of Solon, by which they are no longer governed, that the Naukrari should get in the moneys and make disbursements from the Naukraric funds. He made the Council four hundred, a hundred from each tribe, and he assigned to the council of the Areopagitæ the duty of still watching over the laws generally, just as before it had been the overseer of the administration, and jealously guarded the greater number, and those the most important, of the interests of the citizens, and corrected offenders, having authority to fine and punish, and reported to the state the punishments it inflicted, without recording the reasons of those punishments, and sat in judgment on those who combined for the overthrow of the people, in conformity with Solon's legislation. Now, these were the duties that he assigned in their case. And seeing that the state was often torn by faction, and that some of the citizens from indifference stood aloof, of his own motion he passed a law specially directed against them as follows—that anyone who, when the state was divided into parties, did not take up arms and side with one or the other, should be deprived of his political rights, and have no part in the state.

CHAP. IX.: HOW SOLON GAVE POWER TO THE PEOPLE.

Such, then, were his institutions regarding the officers of state. Now, the following are the three provisions of the constitution of Solon which appear to be the most favourable to the people: first and foremost, the prohibition of loans on the security of the person; then the right accorded to anyone who wished to seek in the courts a remedy for his wrongs; and third (by which, most of all, they say the masses have acquired power), the right of appeal to the court of justice; for when the people is master of the vote, it becomes master of the government. Its power was still further augmented at this time by the want of simplicity in the framing of the laws, and the uncertainty in their interpretation, for as in the case of the law regarding inheritances and only daughters and heiresses, it was inevitable that disputes should arise, and consequently that the courts of law would be the judges in all matters public as well as private. Now, some think that he made his laws uncertain with the express purpose of giving the people some control over the judicial power. Not that this is probable, the explanation rather being that he was unable to embrace in his laws what was best as a general rule and in every particular instance; for it is not right to infer his intention from what is now taking place, but it should be looked for rather in the general spirit of his constitution.

CHAP. X.: REFORMS THE CURRENCY, WEIGHTS AND MEASURES.

In his laws, then, he seems to have introduced these measures in favour of the people, but prior to his legislation to have instituted the cancelling of debts, and afterwards the increase in measures and weights, as well as in the current coin. For it was in his time also that the measures were made larger than the Pheidonean standard, as well as the mina, which had formerly contained about seventy drachmæ. Now, the ancient standard coin was a double drachma. And he made the weight for the current coin sixty(-three) minæ to the talent, and additional minæ were assigned to the stater and all other weights.

CHAP. XI.: GOES ABROAD.

When he had drawn up the constitution in the way that has been described, and everybody came to him and made themselves disagreeable about the laws, some blaming and others criticising, as he did not wish either to disturb these arrangements, or to become an object of hatred by his presence, he determined to go abroad for ten years, proposing to combine trade with observation and to reside in Egypt, in the neighbourhood of the city of Canopus. He came to this determination because he did not think it right that he personally should explain his laws, but his view was that each individual should do what was prescribed by them. It was his ill-fortune too that many of the upper classes had now become his enemies on account of the cancelling of debts, and that both factions had changed their attitude in consequence of the actual settlement proving to be contrary to their expectation. For the people thought that he would make a redistribution of property, and the upper ranks that he would restore again the old order of things. Having disappointed these expectations, he found himself in opposition to both sides, and although it was in his power, by combining with either side, if he wished, to make himself absolute, he chose rather to become an object of hatred to both after he had saved his country and passed the most excellent laws.

CHAP. XII.: THE TESTIMONY OF HIS OWN POEMS.

That this was the position of affairs all without exception agree, and he himself in his poetry refers to it in the following words:

'For to the people I gave such privilege as suffices,
Neither taking away from or aiming at honour.
But such as possessed power, and from their wealth were leaders,
Them I counselled to retain nothing unseemly.
I stood with my mighty shield thrown around both,
And suffered not either to triumph unrighteously.'
And again when expressing his opinion as to how the people ought to be treated:

The people in this way would follow best with its leaders
Under neither too slack nor too strait a control.
For satiety is the parent of insolence, whenever great prosperity follows
Men whose disposition is not well ordered.'

And again, read where he speaks about such as wished to divide the land
among themselves:

'And they came on the spoil with a wealth of hope,
And they thought each of them to find great prosperity,

And that I, though talking smoothly, would manifest a harsh spirit.
Vain were their thoughts then, and now angered with me,
With eyes askance all regard me like enemies.
Not rightly; for what I said, with the help of the gods, I have
accomplished;
But other things I was attempting in vain, nor does it please me
To do aught by force of tyranny, or of our rich fatherland
That the bad should have an equal share with the good.'
And again also about the distress of the poor, and those who were
before in bondage, but were made free by the cancelling of debts:
'But for what reason I the people whirling
On the axle . . . .
She best would bear witness in Time's justice,
Mightiest mother of Olympian gods,
Black Earth, whose boundaries fixed
In many places I formerly plucked up,
She who was before in bondage, but now is free.
And I brought back to Athens, to their god-founded
Fatherland, many who had been sold, one unjustly,

Another justly, and the poor who from necessity
Were exiles, no longer giving utterance to
The Attic tongue, in many directions wandering about;
Those who on this very spot were suffering
Unseemly bondage, trembling at the ways of their masters,
Free I set. This too by the strength
Of law, fitting might and right together.
I wrought and went through with it as I promised.
And laws equally for the good man and the bad,
To each fitting straight justice,
I drew up. Another taking the goad as I did,
An evil-minded and wealth-loving man.

Would not have controlled the people. For if I had wished
What pleased my enemies at that time,

Of many men would this city have been widowed.
For these reasons, girding myself with strength on all sides,
I bore me as a wolf amid many hounds.'
And again, when he reproaches them for the complaints that each side
afterwards levelled against him:
'If it is right to reproach the people plainly,
What they now possess, still sleeping,

They ne'er had looked on with their eyes.
All who are more powerful and in might better
Would commend and claim me as their friend.'
For he says that if ever anybody obtained this honour, he did:
'He would not have controlled the people, or stopt
Before he had disturbed and carried off the beestings;
But I between them in the gap like a barrier
Planted myself.'

CHAP. XIII.: PARTY DIVISIONS IMMEDIATELY FOLLOWING.

These, then, were the reasons why Solon went and lived abroad.

After he had left his country, although the city was still in an unquiet
state, for four years they lived in peace; but in the fifth year after the
magistracy of Solon they did not appoint an archon, owing to the factions
which prevailed; and a second time in the fifth year, for the same reason,
they did not appoint to the office. And after this, in the same period,
Damasias was elected archon, and continued in office for two years and two
months, until he was driven from it by force. Then they decided, on
account of the strength of party feeling, to elect ten archons, five from the
nobles, three from the landowners, and two from the handicraftsmen; and
these held office the year after Damasias, thus making it clear that the
archon possessed the greatest power, for it is evident that they were always
engaged in party strife about this office. And they continued generally in an
unhealthy state in their relations with one another, some on the score of
office, and making a pretext of the cancelling of debts, for they had become
poor men in consequence; some from discontent at the government,
because the change had been great; and others because of their rivalry with
one another. The divisions were three: one the party of the Shore, at the
head of which was Megakles, the son of Alkmæon, and they had the

reputation of aiming, most of all, at a moderate government; and the second, the party of the Plain, who sought an oligarchy, with Lykurgus as their leader; and the third, the party of the Mountain, at the head of which stood Peisistratus, with the character of being a strong partisan of the people. And the ranks of this party had been swollen by such as had been relieved of their debts in consequence of their poverty, and by such as were not of pure blood from motives of fear. *Endnote 006* Evidence of this is afforded by the fact that after the establishment of tyrants they made a proclamation that it was not fitting that many should participate in the government. And each party took its name from the district in which they cultivated the land.

CHAP. XIV.: PEISISTRATUS MAKES HIMSELF TYRANT; HIS EXILE AND RETURN.

Peisistratus, with his character of being a strong partisan of the people and the great reputation that he had made in the war against the Megarians, by covering himself with wounds and then pretending that he had suffered this treatment from the opposite faction, succeeded in persuading the people to give him a body-guard, on the proposal of Aristion. When he had got the club-bearers, as they were called, he rose up with them against the people, and seized the Acropolis in the thirty-second year after the passing of the laws in the archonship of Komeas. The tale goes that Solon, when Peisistratus asked for the guard, spoke against it, and said that he was wiser than some and braver than others; for that he was wiser than all such as did not know that Peisistratus was aiming at absolute power, and braver than such as who, although they knew this, held their peace. When his words availed nothing, taking up his arms before the doors, he said that he had come to the rescue of his country as far as he was able (for he was by this time an exceedingly old man), and called upon everybody else to follow his example. Solon effected nothing at the time by his exhortations. And Peisistratus, after he had possessed himself of the supreme power, administered the state more like a citizen than a tyrant. But as his power was not yet firmly rooted, the parties of Megakles and Lykurgus came to an agreement, and drove him out in the sixth year after his first establishment in the archonship of Hegesias. In the twelfth year after this, Megakles, being harassed by the rival parties, again made proposals to Peisistratus on the condition that he should marry his daughter, and brought him back again in quaint and exceedingly simple fashion. For he first spread a report that Athena was bringing back Peisistratus; then, having found a tall and beautiful woman—as Herodotus says of the deme of the Pæanes, but as some say, a Thracian, a seller of garlands of Kolyttus, whose name was

Phye—he dressed her up so as to look like the goddess, and so brought back the tyrant with him. In this way Peisistratus made his entry, riding in a chariot with the woman sitting by his side, and the citizens, doing obeisance, received them in wonderment.

CHAP. XV.: HOW HE DISARMED THE PEOPLE.

His first return from exile took place in this way. After this, when he was driven out the second time, about the seventh year after his return—for he did not retain his power long, but being unwilling to unite himself to the daughter of Megakles, for fear of giving offence to both factions, went secretly away—he first took part in colonizing a place in the neighbourhood of the Thermæan Gulf, which is called Rhækelus, and thence passed on to the parts about Pangæus. There he made money and hired soldiers, and coming to Eretria in the eleventh year, again he made his first attempt to recover his power by force, with the good-will of many, particularly of the Thebans and Lygdamis of Naxos, besides the knights who were at the head of the government in Eretria. And having been victorious in the battle at Pallene, *Endnote 007* and recovered the supreme power, he stripped the people of their arms, and was now firmly seated in the tyranny. He went to Naxos also and established Lygdamis in power. Now, he stripped the people of their arms after the following fashion: Ordering a review under arms in the Anakeum, he pretended to make an attempt to harangue them, but spoke in a low voice; and when they said they could not hear, he bade them go up to the propylæa of the Acropolis, that he might be heard the better. Whilst he continued addressing them, those who had been appointed for the purpose took away the arms of the people, and shut them up in the neighbouring buildings of the Thesæum. They then came and informed Peisistratus. After finishing his speech, he told the people what had been done about their arms, saying that they had no need to be surprised or out of heart, but bade them go home and attend to their own affairs, adding that all public matters would now be his concern.

CHAP. XVI.: HIS GOVERNMENT MODERATE AND POPULAR.

The tyranny of Peisistratus was at first established in this way, and experienced the changes just enumerated. As we have said, Peisistratus administered the government with moderation, and more like a citizen than a tyrant. For, in applying the laws, he was humane and mild, and towards offenders clement, and, further, he used to advance money to the needy for their agricultural operations, thus enabling them to carry on the cultivation of their lands uninterruptedly. And this he did with two objects: that they might not live in the city, but being scattered over the country, and enjoying moderate means and engaged in their own affairs, they might have neither the desire nor the leisure to concern themselves with public matters. At the same time he had the advantage of a greater revenue from the careful cultivation of the land; for he took a tithe of the produce. It was for this reason, too, that he instituted jurors throughout the demes, and often, leaving the capital, made tours in the country, seeing matters for himself, and reconciling such as had differences, so that they might have no occasion to come to the city and neglect their lands. It was on such a tour that the incident is said to have occurred about the man in Hymettus, who was cultivating what was afterwards called the 'No-Tax-Land.' For seeing a man delving at rocks with a wooden peg and working away, he wondered at his using such a tool, and bade his attendants ask what the spot produced. 'Every ill and every woe under the sun,' replied the man, 'and Peisistratus must take his tithe of these ills and these woes.' Now, the man made this answer not knowing who he was; but Peisistratus, pleased at his boldness of speech and love of work, gave him immunity from all taxes. And he never interfered with the people in any other way indeed during his rule, but ever cultivated peace and watched over it in times of tranquillity. And this is the reason why it often passed as a proverb that the tyranny of Peisistratus was the life of the Golden Age; for it came to pass afterwards, through the insolence of his sons, that the government became much harsher. But what more than any other of his qualities made him a favourite was his popular sympathies and kindness of disposition. For while in all other matters it was his custom to govern entirely according to the laws, so he never allowed himself any unfair advantage, and on one occasion when he was cited before the Areopagus on a charge of murder, he appeared himself in his own defence, and his accuser, getting frightened, withdrew from the suit. It was for such reasons also, that he remained tyrant for a long period, and when he lost his power easily recovered it again; for most of the upper classes and of the popular side desired it, since he helped the one by his intercourse with them, and the other by his assistance in their private affairs, and from his natural disposition could adapt himself to both. The laws of the Athenians regarding tyrants were mild in these times, all of them, and particularly the one relating to any attempt at tyranny, for their law stood as follows: 'These are the ordinances of the Athenians, inherited from their fathers: whoever rises up to make himself a tyrant, or assists in establishing a tyranny, shall be deprived of his political rights, both himself and his family.'

CHAP. XVII.: SUCCEEDED BY HIS SONS.

So Peisistratus retained his power till he became an old man and fell sick and died during the archonship of Philoneos, having lived three-and-thirty years from the time that he first established himself as tyrant. Of this period he continued in power nineteen years, for he was in exile the remainder of the time. It is evident therefore that they talk nonsense who assert that Peisistratus was beloved of Solon, and that he was general in the war with the Megarians about Salamis; for it is impossible from their respective ages, if one calculates how long either lived, and during whose archonship he died. After the death of Peisistratus, his sons held sovereign power, conducting the government in the same way. There were two sons by his wife, Hippias and Hipparchus, and two by the Argive woman, Tophon and Hegesistratus, otherwise called Thessalus. For Peisistratus married from Argos, Timonassa, the daughter of an Argive, whose name was Gorgilus, whom Archinus, the Ampraciot of the Kypselidæ, previously had to wife. From this union arose his friendship with the Argives, and they fought on his side to the number of a thousand at the battle of Pallene, Peisistratus having brought them with him. Some say that he married his Argive wife during his first exile, others that he did so when he was in possession of his power.

CHAP. XVIII.: HARMODIUS AND ARISTOGEITON.

Hippias and Hipparchus were at the head of affairs by right of their claims and their ages; Hippias, being the elder, and by nature fitted for state affairs, and endowed with good sense, presided over the government. But Hipparchus was fond of trifling, amorous, and a votary of the Muses; it was he who sent for Anacreon and Simonides, and the rest of the poets, with their companions. Thessalus was much younger, and in his manner of life overbearing and insolent. And from him came the beginning of all their ills. For being enamoured of Harmodius, and meeting with no response to his affection, he could not restrain his wrath, but took every opportunity of displaying the bitterness of his hatred. At last, when Harmodius' sister was going to act as basket-bearer in the Panathenæa, he forbade her, and made use of some abusive expressions about Harmodius being a coward, the result of which was that Harmodius and Aristogeiton were incited to do their deed in conjunction with many of their fellow-citizens. The celebration of the Panathenæa was proceeding, and they were lying in wait for Hippias on the Acropolis (now, he happened to be following whilst Hipparchus was getting the procession ready), when they saw one of their fellow-conspirators in friendly conversation with Hippias; thinking that he was turning informer, and wishing to do something before they were arrested, they descended from the Acropolis, and without waiting for the rest of the conspirators, killed Hipparchus by the Leokoreum as he was arranging the procession. Thus they ruined the whole plot, and of their number Harmodius was straightway killed by the spearmen, and Aristogeiton was subsequently apprehended, and for a long time subjected to outrage. When he was put to the torture he accused many who were both of illustrious birth and friendly to the tyrants. For it was impossible on the spot to get any clue to the affair, and the story that is told how Hippias disarmed those who were taking part in the procession, and thus caught such as had daggers upon them, is not true; for at that time armed men did not take part in the procession, and the practice was introduced by the people in after-times. And he accused the friends of the tyrants, as the popular side say, on purpose that they might commit an act of impiety, and show their baseness by destroying the guiltless and their own friends; but some say, on the other hand, that it was not an invention on his part, but he informed against such as were actually privy to the plot. And at last, when he was unable, do what he would, to compass his death, he promised to reveal many others, and persuading Hippias to give him his right hand as a pledge of his good faith, as he held it he reviled him for giving his right hand to the murderer of his brother, and so exasperated Hippias that he could not restrain his rage, but drew his sword and despatched him on the spot.

CHAP. XIX.: EXPULSION OF THE PEISISTRATIDÆ.

In consequence of these events the tyranny became much harsher; for both by the vengeance he had taken for his brother, and his many executions and banishments, Hippias had made himself an object of distrust and bitter hatred to all. And about the fourth year after the death of Hipparchus, when things were going badly with him in the city, he took in hand the fortification of Munychia, with the intention of shifting his residence to that quarter. Whilst he was engaged in this work he was driven out by Kleomenes, King of Lacedæmon, as the Laconians were perpetually receiving oracles inciting them to put an end to the tyranny for the following reason. The exiles, at the head of whom were the Alkmæonidæ, were not able by their own unassisted efforts to effect their return, but failed in every attempt; for they were unsuccessful in their intrigues in every instance, and when they fortified Lipsydrium by Parnes, in Attica, where some of their partizans in the city came to join them, they were forced to surrender by the tyrants; hence in later days after this calamity, they used always to sing in their banquet-songs:

'Woe! woe! Lipsydrium, betrayer of thy fellows,
What men hast thou destroyed

Good to fight and good to their native land,
Who then showed of what fathers they were come.'

Failing, then, in all their attempts, they contracted to build the temple at Delphi, by which means they became well supplied with money for procuring the help of the Laconians. For the Pythia was always ordering the Lacedæmonians, when they consulted the oracle, to make Athens free. To this it directly incited the Spartiatæ, although the Peisistratidæ were their friends. And the friendship that subsisted between the Argives and the Peisistratidæ contributed in no less degree to the eagerness of the Laconians. At first, then, they despatched Anchimolus with a force by sea. And after his defeat and death, owing to Kineas the Thessalian having come to the help of the Peisistratidæ with a thousand horse, being further angered by this incident, they despatched Kleomenes their king with a larger force by land. He first gained a victory over the Thessalian horse as they were trying to prevent him from entering Attica, and then shutting up Hippias in what is called the Pelasgic fort, he began to besiege him in conjunction with the Athenians. And as he was blockading it, the sons of the Peisistratidæ happened to be taken prisoners when making a sally. Under these circumstances the Peisistratidæ came to an agreement, stipulating for the safety of their children; and having conveyed away their property within five days, they handed over the Acropolis to the Athenians in the archonship of Harpaktides, having held the tyranny after the death of their father about seventeen years, the whole period, including that of their father's power, amounting to forty-nine years.

CHAP. XX.: ISAGORAS AND KLEISTHENES.

After the tyranny was put down, the parties arrayed against one another were Isagoras the son of Tisandrus, who was a friend of the tyrants, and Kleisthenes, who was of the family of the Alkmæonidæ. Being in a minority in the political clubs, Kleisthenes won over the people by giving political rights to the masses. But Isagoras, not being sufficiently powerful of himself, again called in Kleomenes, who was his friend, and prevailed upon him to help in driving out the pollution, because the Alkmæonidæ were accounted to be among the number of the accursed. And on Kleisthenes secretly withdrawing with a few followers, he drove out as being under the curse seventy households of the Athenians. After this success he made an attempt to overthrow the Council. But when the Council resisted, and the people gathered in crowds, Kleomenes and Isagoras with their followers took refuge in the Acropolis. And the people, blockading it, besieged them for two days, but on the third they let Kleomenes and all his followers depart on certain terms, and sent for Kleisthenes and the rest of the exiles. When the people had made itself master of the government, Kleisthenes became the leader and representative of the people. For the expulsion of the tyrants was almost entirely due to the Alkmæonidæ, and they continued for the most part to carry on a party warfare. But even before the Alkmæonidæ, Kedon made an attack on the tyrants, and for that reason they used to sing about him also at banquets:

'By spear and Kedon, boy, and forget not,
If it is thine to pour out wine to brave men.'

CHAP. XXI.: THE CONSTITUTION OF KLEISTHENES.

These then were the reasons why the people had confidence in Kleisthenes. And at that time, when he was at the head of the masses, in the fourth year after the overthrow of the tyrants, he first distributed them all into ten tribes instead of four as previously, wishing to mix them up in order that more might have a share in the government; hence the saying, 'not to examine the tribes,' as addressed to those who wished to review the lists of the families. *Endnote 008* Afterwards he made the Council five hundred instead of four hundred, taking fifty from each tribe, for at that time there were a hundred from each tribe. And the reason why he did not distribute them into twelve tribes was that he might not have to divide them according to the existing Trittyes (third parts of tribes); for the four tribes were composed of twelve Trittyes, with the result that the masses were not intermingled. And he divided the country by demes into thirty parts, ten for the neighbourhood of the city, ten for the shore districts, and ten for the interior, and calling these Trittyes, he allotted three to each tribe, that each might have a part in all the different localities. And he made fellow-members of the same deme those who lived in each of the demes, in order that they might not, by calling after the name of the father, detect the new citizens, but give them their surnames from their demes; hence it is that the Athenians do call themselves by their demes. He also established presidents of the demes, with the same duties as the former Naukrari; for he also made the demes take the place of the Naukrariæ. And he named some of the demes from their localities, and others from their founders; since some of the localities now erected into demes had no founders from whom they could be called. *Endnote 009* But the Genē (collections of families) and Phratriæ (three to a tribe, and comprising each thirty Genē) and the priesthoods he

18

allowed each to retain as they had come down to them from their forefathers. And to the tribes he gave surnames from the hundred selected founders whom the Pythia appointed, to the number of ten.

CHAP. XXII.: THE TIMES IMMEDIATELY FOLLOWING; OSTRACISM; BUILDING OF A HUNDRED TRIREMES.

In consequence of these changes the constitution became much more popular than that of Solon; for it had come to pass that under the tyranny the laws of Solon had become a dead letter from disuse, and that Kleisthenes had made the others to win over the masses, among which was passed the law about ostracism. First then in the fifth year after this settlement, in the archonship of Hermoukreon they drew up for the Council of the five hundred the oath by which they swear even to this day; then they chose the generals by tribes, from each tribe one, and the polemarch was the commander-in-chief. In the twelfth year after this, when they had been victorious at Marathon, in the archonship of Phænippus, and two years had elapsed since the victory, and the people had now grown bold, then it was that for the first time they put in force the law about ostracism. Now this law had been passed by reason of their suspicion of those in power, because Peisistratus had established himself as tyrant when he was a leader of the people and a general. The very first man to be ostracised was one of his relations, Hipparchus, the son of Charmus of Kolyttus, on whose account especially it was that Kleisthenes, wishing to get him banished, passed the law. For the Athenians allowed all the friends of the tyrants, who had not taken any part in wrong-doing during the troubles, to live in the city, thus displaying the wonted clemency of the popular government. Of these Hipparchus was the leader and representative. At the beginning of the following year, in the archonship of Telesinus, they appointed by lot the nine archons according to tribes from the five hundred, who had been selected by the members of demes immediately after the tyranny (for formerly they had been all elected). And Megakles, the son of Hippocrates of Alopeke, was ostracised. For three years then they kept ostracising the friends of the tyrants, and after this in the fourth year they removed anyone else besides who appeared to be too powerful. The first to be ostracised of those who were not connected with the tyranny was Xanthippus, the son of Ariphron. And in the third year after this, during the archonship of Nicodemus, when the mines at Maronea were discovered, and the state acquired a hundred talents from working them, some counselled the people to divide the money among themselves. But Themistokles would not allow it, declaring that he would not use the money, and urged them to advance it on loan to the hundred richest men among the Athenians, to each a talent, and then recommended, if it met their approval, that it should be expended in the service of the state, and if not, that they should get in the money from those who had borrowed it. Getting the money in this way, he had a hundred triremes built, each of the hundred talents building one; and it was with these ships that they fought at Salamis against the barbarians. In these times Aristides, the son of Lysimachus, was ostracised. And in the fourth year, in the archonship of Hypsichides, they received back all who had been ostracised, in consequence of Xerxes' expedition. And for the future they made Geræstus and Scyllæum the prescribed limits within which ostracised persons were free to live, and in default they were to lose their political rights for ever.

CHAP. XXIII.: RECOVERY OF POWER BY THE AREOPAGUS; THEMISTOKLES AND ARISTIDES.

At that time, then, and up to this point in its history, the state advanced together with the democracy, and gradually increased in power. But after the Median war the council of the Areopagus again became powerful, and administered the government, having got the leadership, not from any formal decree, but from having brought about the sea-fight at Salamis. For when the generals had shown themselves quite unequal to the emergency, and had proclaimed a sauve qui peut, the Areopagus came forward with funds, and distributing eight drachmæ to each sailor, so manned the ships. For this reason they yielded to its claims, and the Athenians were governed well at this particular period; for circumstances led them to give their attention to war: they were held in high esteem among the Greeks, and made themselves masters of the sea, despite the Lacedæmonians. The leaders of the people in these days were Aristides, the son of Lysimachus, and Themistokles, the son of Neokles, the latter devoting himself to military matters, while the former enjoyed the reputation of being a sagacious statesman, and conspicuous for justice among his contemporaries. They accordingly made use of the services of the one in war, and of the other in council. The rebuilding of the walls, however, was conducted by both of them together, notwithstanding their political differences; but it was Aristides who urged on the revolt of the Ionians and the alliance with the Lacedæmonians, watching his opportunity when the Laconians had been brought into ill-odour by the doings of Pausanias. This was the reason why it was he who apportioned to the cities the tributes which were first imposed in the third year after the sea-fight at Salamis in the archonship of Timosthenes, and why he made a treaty with the Ionians,

20

offensive and defensive, in confirmation of which they sunk the bars of iron in the sea. *Endnote 010*

CHAP. XXIV.: ATHENS LAYS CLAIMS TO THE LEADERSHIP OF GREECE.

After this, when the city was now in good heart and its treasury overflowing, he advised the people to lay a claim to national supremacy, and to leave the country, and come and live in the city; saying that there would be the means of living for all, for some in military service, for others in keeping guard, and for the rest in public employments, and that in this way they would obtain national supremacy. Yielding to these representations, they assumed the leadership of Greece, and treated the allies in sufficiently lordly fashion, except the Chians and Lesbians and Samians; for these they kept as guards of their empire, leaving them their forms of government, and not interfering with their rule over such subjects as they had. They established for the masses easy means of subsistence, just in the way Aristides had shown them; for from their tributes and their taxes and their allies the maintenance of more than twenty thousand men was provided. There were six thousand jurors, and sixteen hundred archers, and in addition to them twelve hundred cavalry, five hundred of the Council, and guards of the dockyards five hundred, and in the city fifty guards, and home magistrates up to seven hundred men, and men on foreign service up to seven hundred; and besides these, when they afterwards engaged in war, two thousand five hundred hoplites, and twenty guard-ships, and other ships which brought the tributes, manned by two thousand men chosen by lot, and further the Prytaneum, and orphans and guards of prisoners; for all these derived their maintenance from the public funds.

CHAP. XXV.: OVERTHROW OF THE AREOPAGUS BY EPHIALTES AND THEMISTOKLES.

The people therefore got its means of support in this way. And for about seventeen years after the Persian war the constitution was maintained under the presidency of the Areopagitæ, although it was gradually losing ground. But as the masses were increasing in power, Ephialtes, the son of Sophonides, with the reputation of being incorruptible and of entertaining just intentions towards the constitution, became leader of the people, and made an attack on the council. First he made away with many of the Areopagitæ, bringing actions against them for their administration. Afterwards, in the archonship of Konon, he stripped the council of all the privileges, in right of which it was the guardian of the constitution, and made them over partly to the five hundred and partly to the courts of justice. And he carried out these measures in conjunction with Themistokles, who was one of the Areopagitæ, and about to be put on his trial on the charge of Medism. And desiring the overthrow of the council, Themistokles told Ephialtes that the council intended to seize him as well as himself, while at the same time he told the Areopagitæ that he would point out to them those who were banding together for the overthrow of the government. And taking the persons who were despatched by the council to the house of Ephialtes, to point out to them those who were meeting together there, he joined in earnest conversation with the representatives of the council. And Ephialtes, seeing this, in alarm took refuge at the altar with only his tunic on. All wondered at what had happened, and when the Council of the five hundred assembled afterwards, Ephialtes and Themistokles brought accusations against the Areopagitæ, and again before the people in the same way, until they stripped them of their power. And Ephialtes also was got rid of, being treacherously murdered not long afterwards by Aristodicus of Tanagra. So the council of the Areopagitæ was in this way deprived of its supervision of the state.

CHAP. XXVI.: GROWTH OF THE DEMOCRACY; KIMON.

After this, in the course of circumstances, the constitution became further weakened through the zeal of the leaders of the people, for in these times, as it fell out, the more moderate party was without a leader. Now Kimon, the son of Miltiades, was at their head, a man comparatively young, and who had entered upon public life late. Moreover, the greater portion of this party had been destroyed in war, which happened in this way: The army was enrolled in those times from those who were on the list for service, and generals were appointed to command who had no experience of war, but were held in honour for their ancestral glories, the consequence of which was, that those who went to the wars perished by two or three thousand at a time. In this way the moderate men, both of the people and of the well-to-do, were used up. Now, in everything else the government was administered differently to what it was before, when men gave heed to the laws, but the election of the nine archons was not disturbed. Still, in the sixth year after the death of Ephialtes, they decreed that those who were to be balloted for in the elections of the nine archons should be selected also from the Zeugitæ, and the first of that class who filled the office was Mnesitheides. But all before him had belonged to the Knights and Pentakosiomedimni, while the Zeugitæ used to hold the offices that went round in succession (but not the archonship), unless some oversight of the provisions of the laws chanced to occur. In the fifth year after this, in the archonship of Lysikrates, the thirty jurors were again established, who were called after the demes. In the third year after him, in the archonship of Antidotus, owing to the great increase in the number of citizens, they decreed, on the proposal of Perikles, that no one should share in political rights unless both his parents were citizens.

CHAP. XXVII.: PERIKLES.

After this Perikles came to lead the people. He first made a name for himself when, as a young man, he called in question the accounts of Kimon during his command. The constitution then became, in the course of events, still more democratical; for he stripped the Areopagitæ of some of their privileges, and, what was the cardinal point of his policy, urged on the state to acquire naval power, in consequence of which the masses grew bold, and drew the whole government more into their own hands. And in the forty-ninth year after the seafight at Salamis, in the archonship of Pythodorus, the Peloponnesian war broke out, during which the people, shut up as they were in the city and accustomed to serve for pay in the armies, partly of their own free will, and partly against their wishes, elected to administer the government themselves. And Perikles was the first to introduce pay for the services of the jurors, thus bidding for popularity as against the influence that Kimon derived from his ample means. For Kimon, as the possessor of royal wealth, first discharged the public services with great splendour, and afterwards supported many of the members of his deme. Any of the Lakiadæ who liked might go to him every day to get their rations; moreover, all his grounds were left unfenced, so that anyone who liked could help himself to the fruit. But as Perikles did not possess the means of indulging in public expenditure of this kind, on the advice of Damonides of Œa (who had the reputation of being the prompter of Perikles' wars, for which reason also they ostracised him later), since his private property did not allow him to provide subsistence for the populace, he instituted pay for the jurors. And to these causes some assign the deterioration in the conduct of affairs, as the appointments to office were designedly made more and more by haphazard instead of by merit. And bribery in the law courts also began to be practised after this, Anytus being the first to show how to do it after his command at Pylos; for when he was put upon his trial for losing it, he bribed the court and was acquitted.

CHAP. XXVIII.: HIS SUCCESSORS; NIKIAS, KLEON, THUCYDIDES, THERAMENES.

So long then as Perikles was at the head of the people, the government went on better, but on his death it became much worse. For then, for the first time, the people took for its leader a man who was not held in respect by such as entertained moderate views; whereas in former times it had always, without exception, been led by men of character. For it began with Solon, who was the first to come forward as the leader of the people; and next Peisistratus, who belonged to the nobles and upper class; and after the overthrow of the tyranny came Kleisthenes, who was of the house of the Alkmæonidæ, and had no party-leader in opposition to him after the banishment of Isagoras and his faction. After this Xanthippus was at the head of the people, while Miltiades represented the upper classes. Next came Themistokles and Aristides; after them Ephialtes was at the head of the democratic party, and Kimon, the son of Miltiades, at the head of the wealthy classes. Then Perikles represented the democratic party, and Thucydides, who was a connection by marriage of Kimon, the other side. On the death of Perikles, Nikias took the lead of the nobles, he who met his end in Sicily; and of the democratic party, Kleon, the son of Kleænetus. He has the reputation of having, more than any other man, led the people astray by his impetuosity, and was the first to raise his voice to a shriek from the rostra and indulge in abusive language, and to harangue with his apron on, while everybody else respected the ordinary decencies of public speaking. After them Theramenes, the son of Hagnon, led the other side, while at the head of the people was Kleophon, the lyre-maker, who first introduced the payment of the two obols. For some time he distributed it, but afterwards Kallikrates, the Pæanian, put a stop to it, having first promised that he would add another obol to the two obols. Later on they were both condemned to death; for it is the custom of the masses, when they discover that they have been grossly deceived, to hate those who have led them on to do anything that is not right. And from Kleophon onward the leadership of the people successively passed without interruption to such men as were the most willing to act boldly and gratify the populace, looking only to the immediate present. For of those who conducted the government at Athens, and succeeded to the old rulers, Nikias and Thucydides and Theramenes appear to have approved themselves the best. In the case of Nikias and Thucydides almost all agree that they showed themselves to be not only good and honourable men, but also fit to govern, and that they administered the state in every respect in conformity with the national traditions. With regard to Theramenes, however, as disturbances in the forms of government occurred in his time, opinions differ. Still, he seems to such as do not express a mere off-hand opinion, not to have overthrown all these forms, as his accusers charge him with doing, but to have carried on all of them so long as they did not contravene the laws; thus acting like a man who was able to live under any form of government, which is indeed the duty of a good citizen, but who would not be a party to any that was contrary to the law, and so he became an object of hatred.

CHAP. XXIX.: THE FOUR HUNDRED; THE PROPOSALS OF PYTHODORUS.

So long, then, as successes in the war were evenly balanced, they preserved the democracy. But after the reverse in Sicily, when the Lacedæmonians became very powerful by their alliance with the king of Persia, they were compelled to change the democracy and establish the government of the four hundred, on the proposal of Melobius before the decree and Pythodorus moving . . . the masses being influenced, beyond all other considerations, by the idea that the king would gladly take part with them in the war if they made the government oligarchical. Now, the decree of Pythodorus was as follows: that the people should choose, in conjunction with the standing committee of ten, twenty others from such as were above forty years of age, and that they, after swearing solemnly to pass such measures as they might think best for the state, should so legislate for its safety; and that it should be lawful for anyone else who wished to bring forward any bill, that so, out of all, they might choose what was best. And Kleitophon spoke to the same effect as Pythodorus, but moved further that those who were elected should examine the long-established laws which Kleisthenes passed when he established the democracy, that by listening to them also they might decide on what was best, for they argued that Kleisthenes' constitution was not democratic, but on the same lines as that of Solon. After their election they first moved that it should be compulsory on the presidents of the Council to put to the vote all proposals about the safety of the state; then they did away with indictments for proposing unconstitutional measures, and in cases not provided for by law, and legal challenges, so that any Athenian who wished might assist in the deliberations about the matters before them. They proposed, further, that if anyone, on account of these proceedings, should fine or summons anyone, or bring a case into court, an information should be laid against him, and he should be brought before the generals, and the generals should hand him over to the Eleven to be punished with death. After this they drew up the constitution as follows: that it should not be lawful to expend the incoming moneys for any other purpose than the war, and that all offices should be held without pay so long as the war might last, with the exception of the nine archons and the presidents of the Council for the time being, but that these should receive three obols a day each. They proposed, further, to vest all the rest of the administration in such of the Athenians as were best able both in person and means to perform the public services, to the number of not less than five thousand, so long as the war might last; that they should have the power also of making treaties with whomever they liked; and that the committee should choose ten men from each tribe over forty years of age to enrol the five thousand, after having taken an oath on perfect sacrifices.

CHAP. XXX.: THE CONSTITUTION AS PROPOSED FOR THE FUTURE.

Those who were appointed, then, drew up these measures. And after their ratification the five thousand chose a hundred out of their own number to make a public record of the form of government. So this body drew up and published the following record. Such as were over thirty years of age were to be members of the Council for a year, without pay; and from them were to be appointed the generals and the nine archons and the sacred recorder, and the infantry and cavalry commanders, and the chiefs of the tribes, the commandants of the forts, the treasurers of the sacred funds of Athena and all other gods to the number of ten, the Hellenotamiæ, *Endnote 011* and the treasurers of all other sacred funds to the number of twenty, who were to control the managers of sacred rites and superintendents, each ten in number; and they were to choose all the above out of selected candidates, who at the expiration of their term should select successors from the then members of the Council, but all the other officers were to be appointed by lot, and not from the Council; and such of the Hellenotamiæ as might be managing the funds were not to take part in the Council. Further, that they should constitute four councils from the aforesaid age for the future, and of these the division to whose lot it fell should act as Council, and it should appoint also the rest to act according to each lot. That the hundred (who were drawing up the constitution) should apportion both themselves and the others into four divisions, as fairly as possible, and appoint them in turn by lot, and they should form the Council for a year. That they should recommend such measures as appeared likely to them to be the best in regard to the public money, with a view to its safe-keeping and expenditure on what was necessary, and about everything else as best they could; further, if they should wish to take counsel on any matter in a larger body than their own, each of them should call in to his assistance any assessor he liked from such as were of the same age. That they should make the sittings of the Council once every five days, unless they required more. That the Council should appoint by lot the nine archons, but that they should select by vote five who had been appointed by lot out of the Council, and out of them one should be appointed by lot every day to put the question. That the before-mentioned five should appoint by lot those who wished to present themselves before the Council, first regarding sacred matters, next for the heralds, thirdly for embassage, and fourthly about all other matters. That the generals should have the management of matters connected with the war department, whenever it might be necessary to make any proposal without casting lots. Lastly, that anyone who failed to be present at the appointed hour in the chamber of the Council when it was sitting, should pay a fine of a drachma for each day, unless he had obtained leave of absence from the Council.

CHAP. XXXI.: THE CONSTITUTION AS PROPOSED FOR THE IMMEDIATE PRESENT.

Such was the constitution they drew up to serve for the future; but for the immediate present its provisions were as follows: That the Council should consist of four hundred as instituted by their fathers, forty from each tribe, from such candidates as the tribesmen might select above thirty years of age. That they should appoint the officers of state, draw up the form of oath to be taken, and do whatever they judged expedient concerning the laws and audits of accounts and everything else. That they should govern by the established laws regarding matters of state, and should not have the right of altering them or passing different ones. For the present they should make choice of the generals out of the whole body of the five thousand, and the Council, after its appointment, should hold a review under arms, and should choose ten men and a secretary for them; these on their election were to hold office for the coming year with full powers, and, as occasion might require, concert measures in common with the Council. That they should choose one commander of cavalry and ten chiefs of tribes; *Endnote 012* but for the future the Council was to make choice of them in conformity with the written law. In respect of all other offices, except the Council and the generals, it should not be lawful for them or anyone else to hold the same office more than once. And for the remainder of the time the four hundred should be distributed into the four lots . . . .

CHAP. XXXII.: THE GOVERNMENT OF THE FOUR HUNDRED.

So the hundred who were chosen by the five hundred drew up this constitution. When its provisions, on the motion of Aristomachus, had been ratified by the masses, the Council was dissolved in the archonship of Kallias before it had completed its term, on the 14th of the month Thargelion, *Endnote 013* and the four hundred entered on office on the 21st of Thargelion, while the Council elected by lot ought to have entered on office on the 14th of Skirophorion. The oligarchy then was established in this way in the archonship of Kallias, about a hundred years after the expulsion of the tyrants, its establishment being mainly due to Peisander, Antiphon and Theramenes, men of good antecedents, and with a character for intelligence and prudence. On the introduction of this form of government the five thousand were only nominally appointed, but the four hundred, in conjunction with the ten who were invested with full powers, entering the council-chamber, assumed the management of affairs. Sending an embassy to the Lacedæmonians, they proposed putting an end to the war on the terms that each side should retain what they held, but withdrew from further negotiation when the Lacedæmonians refused to listen to any proposal which did not include the surrender of their maritime supremacy.

CHAP. XXXIII.: IT LASTED FOUR MONTHS, AND WAS GOOD.

The government of the four hundred lasted about four months, and of this body Mnasilochus was archon for the space of two months during the archonship of Theopompus, *Endnote 014* who held office the remaining two months. But after the defeat in the sea-fight at Eretria, and the revolt of the whole of Eubœa except Oreus, being more incensed at this calamity than at any that had ever hitherto befallen them (for Eubœa was of greater advantage to them than Attica), the Athenians put down the four hundred, and gave the management of affairs to the five thousand under arms (referred to above), after passing a vote that anyone who received pay should be ineligible for offices of state. The overthrow of the four hundred was mainly due to Aristokrates and Theramenes, who did not approve of their doings, for they managed everything themselves, without ever referring to the five thousand. But the administration seems to have been good at this time, considering that a war was being carried on, and that the form of government was a military one.

CHAP. XXXIV.: ARGINUSÆ ÆGOSPOTAMI LYSANDER AND ESTABLISHMENT OF THE OLIGARCHY.

However, the people quickly stripped them of their power; for in the seventh year from the overthrow of the four hundred, in the archonship of Kallias of Angele, after the sea-fight at Arginusæ, it happened, in the first place, that the ten victorious generals of the sea-fight were all condemned by one vote, though some of them had not even taken part in the battle, and others were themselves saved on another vessel, for the people had been grossly deluded by those who had worked upon its angry mood. And, secondly, when the Lacedæmonians wished to retire from Dekelea and return home and conclude peace on the terms that each side should retain what they held, some were anxious for it, but the masses would not listen to the proposal, grossly deluded as they were by Kleophon, who prevented peace from being made. He came to the assembly drunk and with his breastplate on, declaring that he would not allow it unless the Lacedæmonians gave up all the cities. And when things did not prosper with them, no long time after they discovered their mistake; for in the following year, in the archonship of Alexias, befell the disastrous seafight at Ægospotami, the result of which was that Lysander made himself master of the government, and established the thirty in the following manner. When they had made peace on the condition that they should live under the form of government which they had inherited from their fathers, on the one hand the popular side was trying to preserve the democracy; while on the other, of the upper classes such as belonged to the political clubs, and the exiles who had returned after the peace, were desirous of an oligarchy, and those who were not members of any club, but otherwise had the character of being inferior to none of their fellow-citizens, were seeking for the form of government inherited from their fathers. Amongst this number were Archinus, Anytus, Kleitophon, Phormisios, and several others, and at the head of them Theramenes was conspicuous. When Lysander attached himself to the oligarchs, the people were terror-stricken and compelled to vote for the oligarchy. Drakontides of Aphidnæ proposed the vote.

CHAP. XXXV.: THE THIRTY AND THEIR GOVERNMENT.

So the thirty were established in this way in the archonship of Pythodorus. Being now masters of the state, they neglected all the other provisions regarding the government, and appointed only the five hundred members of the Council, and the other magistrates from selected candidates out of the thousand; and taking to themselves ten governors of Peiræus, and eleven guards of the prison, and three hundred attendants furnished with scourges, they kept the government in their own hands. At first they behaved with moderation to their fellow-citizens, and affected to administer the government as inherited from their fathers. They annulled in the Areopagus the laws of Ephialtes and Archestratus regarding the Areopagitæ, and such of Solon's laws as were of doubtful interpretation, and put down the supreme authority vested in the jurors, as if they were going to restore the constitution, and remove all doubts in its interpretation. For example, in the matter of a man's giving his own property to whom he likes, they gave him full authority once for all; and they removed such difficulties as might arise, except on the grounds of mental aberration, old age, or undue female influence, so that no door might be left open to common informers; in all other cases they proceeded in like manner and with the same object. At first then such was their line of action, and they made away with the common informers and such as associated themselves with the people to do its pleasure in opposition to its true interests, and were mischievous and bad. And men rejoiced at these doings, thinking that they were actuated by the best motives. But when they had got a firmer grip of power, not a single individual did they spare, but killed alike such as were distinguished for their wealth, birth, or rank, getting rid in this underhand way of those whom they were afraid of, and whose property, at the same time, they wished to plunder. By such means they had succeeded within a short period in making away with not less than fifteen hundred persons.

CHAP. XXXVI.: PROTESTS OF THERAMENES.

When the state was drifting in this way, Theramenes, indignant at their proceedings, exhorted them to put a stop to such outrages and give a share of the administration to the best men. They at first resisted, but when reports spread among the people, who were for the most part well disposed to Theramenes, then, fearing that he might constitute himself the champion of the people and put an end to their power, they drew up a list of three thousand citizens, declaring that they would give them a share in the government. Theramenes again found fault with this arrangement, on the following grounds: first, that although they professed a desire to give a share of their power to respectable citizens, they proposed to do so with three thousand only, just as if worth were limited to that number; secondly, that they were acting in a way which was in the highest degree inconsistent, by establishing a government which was a government of force and yet inferior in power to the governed. But they made light of these objections, and for a long time held back the list of the three thousand, keeping their names a secret; and when they did think good to publish them, they cancelled some on the list and substituted others who had not been originally included.

CHAP. XXXVII.: THERAMENES PUT TO DEATH, AND THE LACEDÆMONANS CALL ED IN.

When winter had now set in, and Thrasybulus and the exiles had seized Phyle, the thirty, having fared badly with the army which they had led out against them, determined to strip everybody else of their arms and destroy Theramenes after the following manner: They brought forward two measures in the Council and ordered it to pass them; one was to invest the thirty with full powers to put to death any citizen whose name was not on the list of the three thousand; the other to deprive of their political rights all who had taken part in the destruction of the fort in Eetionæa, or had in any way acted in opposition to the four hundred, or the founders of the former oligarchy. Now the fact was that Theramenes had had a share in both, with the consequence that when these proposals had been passed he was put in the position of an outlaw, and the thirty had the power of putting him to death. So, after making away with Theramenes, they stripped every one of his arms except the three thousand, and in every way indulged freely in cruelty and evil-doing. Sending ambassadors to Lacedæmon, they brought accusations against Theramenes, and asked for help, in compliance with which the Lacedæmonians despatched Kallibius as governor (Harmost), with about seven hundred men, who on their arrival garrisoned the Acropolis.

CHAP. XXXVIII.: END OF THE THIRTY, AND RECONCILIATION OF PARTIES.

After this, when the exiles from Phyle had seized Munychia and been victorious in an engagement over the force that had come to its help with the thirty, the citizens, retiring after the attempt, and assembling on the morrow in the market-place, put down the thirty, and appointed ten of the citizens, with full powers, to bring the war to an end. Now they, after taking over the government, did not enter into the negotiations for which they had been appointed, but sent an embassy to Lacedæmon, asking for help and borrowing money. When those who had a voice in the government were displeased at this, fearing that they might be deposed from power, and wishing to strike terror into the rest—as, indeed, they did—they seized and put to death . . . a man second to none of the citizens, and, with the help of Kallibius and his Peloponnesians, and besides them some of the knights, got a firm hold of the government. Now some of the knights were more anxious than any of their fellow-citizens that the exiles at Phyle should not return. When, however, the forces which held the Peiræus and Munychia, to which all the popular party had withdrawn, were getting the better in the war, then they put down the ten who were first appointed and chose ten others of the highest character, during whose government was accomplished both the reconciliation and the return of the popular party with their zealous co-operation. Notably at their head stood Rhinon the Pæanian, and Phaÿllus, the son of Acherdes; they indeed, both before the arrival of Pausanias, were in constant negotiation with the party at Peiræus, and after his arrival actively assisted him in bringing about their return. For the peace was concluded as well as the reconciliation by Pausanias, king of the Lacedæmonians, in conjunction with the ten mediators, who afterwards arrived from Lacedæmon, and were sent at his urgent request. And Rhinon and his party found favour from their goodwill towards the popular party, and although they assumed charge under an oligarchy, they handed over the scrutiny of accounts to the democracy, and no one brought any charge against them, either of those who had remained in the city or come back from Peiræus; on the contrary, in recognition of their services Rhinon was immediately appointed general.

CHAP. XXXIX.: TERMS OF THE RECONCILIATION.

Now, the reconciliation was effected in the archonship of Eukleides on the following terms: Such Athenians as had remained in the city and wished to leave it might live at Eleusis without forfeiting their rights, and with full authority and powers in all their affairs and the enjoyment of their property. The temple should be common to both, and under the charge of the heralds and Eumolpidæ in conformity with the ancient customs. It should not be lawful for such as were at Eleusis to go to the city, nor for those in the city to go to Eleusis, except for the mysteries. They should contribute from their incomes to the alliance just like the other Athenians. And if any of these who went away took a house at Eleusis, they should get the assent of the owner; and if they failed to agree about terms, they should choose three appraisers on either side, and he should take the price which they fixed. Any Eleusinians they liked might live with them. The registry for those who wanted to live away should be as follows: for such as were at home from the day they took the oath, a space of seven days and twenty days for the departure, and for those who were away after they had come back again, the same conditions. It should not be lawful for anyone living at Eleusis to hold any office in the city before he was registered again as living in the city. Trials for murder should be according to the ancient customs; if anyone killed another with his own hand he should pay the penalty, after making his offering. The act of amnesty should be binding on everyone, except as against the thirty and the ten and the Eleven and the late magistrates of Peiræus, and that not even these should be excluded if they submitted their accounts. The magistrates of Peiræus should render accounts of matters done in Peiræus, and the city magistrates in matters concerned with rateable valuations. When affairs were arranged in this way, such as wished should live away. Lastly, each side should repay separately the money they had borrowed for the war.

CHAP. XL.: ITS CONCLUSION; ACTION OF ARCHINUS.

The reconciliation being concluded on these terms, all who had sided with the thirty got alarmed, and many who intended to leave put off their registry to the last days, as everybody does in such cases. Looking at the largeness of their number, and wishing to stop them, Archinus took away the remaining days of registry, so that many were compelled to remain, though against their will, till they regained confidence. In so doing Archinus seems to have acted like a wise statesman, as well as on a later occasion when he denounced as unlawful the decree of Thrasybulus, by which he was for giving political rights to all those who had returned together from Peiræus, since some of them were undoubtedly slaves. In a third instance also he showed his wisdom, when he brought before the Council the first of the restored exiles who had violated the act of amnesty and secured his summary execution, arguing that they had now an opportunity of showing if they intended to maintain the democracy and abide by their oaths, for that if they let this man go they would give encouragement to the rest, but if they put him to death they would make him an example to all. Now, this was just what did come to pass, for on his being put to death nobody ever afterwards violated the amnesty. At the same time they seem in all that they did to have treated their late calamities in the most excellent and statesmanlike way, both individually and as members of the community. For not only did they wholly forego the memory of past wrongs, but they repaid in common to the Lacedæmonians the money which the thirty had got for the war, although their agreement provided that each side, the city and Peiræus, should pay separately. They considered such action to be the startingpoint of unity, whereas in every other state a victorious democracy not only does not contribute out of its own pockets more than it is obliged, but even makes a new distribution of the land. Finally, a reconciliation was effected with such as were living at Eleusis, in the third year after their leaving, in the archonship of Xenænetus.

CHAP. XLI.: RECAPITULATION OF THE PRECEDING CHANGES; THE SOVEREIGN POWER OF THE PEOPLE.

This was the course of events at the later period, but at that time the people, having made itself master of the state, established the form of government as it now exists, in the archonship of Pythodorus. And it appears that the people rightly assumed the supreme authority by reason of its having accomplished unaided the return of the exiles. This change was the eleventh in order. First came the constitution of those who united them into one people at the beginning, viz., Ion and his followers; for it was then for the first time that they were distributed as one people into the four tribes, and that the tribe-kings were appointed. The next and first remarkable form of government after this was that which took shape in the time of Theseus, varying but slightly from the kingly form. After this Draco's, in which the laws also were first recorded in writing. Thirdly, Solon's, after the civil discords, from which dates the beginning of the democracy. Fourthly, the tyranny of Peisistratus. Fifthly, after the overthrow of the tyrants, the constitution of Kleisthenes, more democratic than Solon's. The sixth was after the Persian war, when the council of Areopagus presided over the state. Seventh, and following the preceding, was that which Aristides sketched out, and Ephialtes completed, by putting down the Areopagitic council; it was under this constitution that the state, under the leadership of the demagogues, made very many mistakes by reason of its maritime supremacy. The eighth was the constitution of the four hundred, and after this, and ninth, the democracy again. The tenth was the tyranny of the thirty and that of the ten. Eleventh, that after the return of the exiles from Phyle and Peiræus, which from its establishment up to the present day has continued uninterruptedly to add further to the power of the masses. For the people itself has made itself master of everything, and administers everything according to its views by its decrees and by its control of the courts of justice, in which it is the supreme power, for even the decisions of the Council come before the people. In this, indeed, they seem to act rightly, for a few are more open to corruption both by bribes and favours than the masses. Now, at first they decided against payment to the Assembly, but when people would not attend it and the presidents had to pass many measures, to secure the presence of the masses for the confirmation of the voting, first Agyrrhius made the pay an obol, and after

34

him Herakleides of Klazomenæ, surnamed the king, two obols, and again Agyrrhius made it three obols.

CHAP. XLII.: ADMISSION TO CITIZENSHIP; TRAINING OF THE EPHEBI.

The present constitution is as follows: Political rights belong to those whose parents are citizens on both sides. When they are eighteen years old they are enrolled as members of their deme. When a candidate is proposed, the members of the deme decide by vote about him on oath; first, if they consider him to be of the proper legal age; if they decide against it, he returns to the class of children; and secondly, if he is freeborn and his birth according to the laws. Then, if they decide that he is not freeborn, the candidate appeals to the court of justice, and the members of the deme choose of their number five plaintiffs, and if it is decided that he is not rightly enrolled, the state sells him; but if he gains the day, it is compulsory on the deme to enrol him as a member. After this the Council examines the candidates who have been enrolled, and if any is found to be less than eighteen years old, it fines the members of the deme who enrolled him. When they have passed as Ephebi (i.e., arrived at man's estate), their fathers assemble in their tribes, and on oath select three of their tribesmen above forty years of age, whom they consider to be most worthy and suitable to have charge of the Ephebi, and from them the people votes one of each tribe, selected as their moderator and superintendent in everything from the whole body of Athenians. And, taking charge of the Ephebi, first they make a circuit of the sacred places, then they proceed to Peiræus, and some of the Ephebi garrison Munychia, and the rest the shore. The people votes them also two gymnastic-masters and teachers, who instruct them in the use of arms, shooting, hurling, and working the catapult. It gives for maintenance to the moderators a drachma a day each, and to the Ephebi four obols each. And each moderator, taking the money of his own tribesmen, buys what is necessary for all in common (for they take their meals together by their tribes), and provides for everything else. They pass their first year in this way. The next, at a meeting of the Assembly in the theatre, they display before the people their drill-practice, and receiving a spear and shield from the state, patrol the country and live in garrisons. They act as guards for their two years, wearing cloaks, and have immunity from all public burdens. They are not allowed either to bring or defend an action, to prevent their being connected in any way with business, except in cases of inheritance and of an only daughter and heiress, or where a question of family priesthood arises. On the expiry of the two years they at once rank with the rest. Such, then, are the regulations regarding the enrolment of citizens and the Ephebi.

CHAP. XLIII.: ELECTION TO OFFICES, BY LOT OR VOTE.

They appoint by lot to all the offices belonging to the administration which comes round in turn, except the military treasurer, and those who have charge of the funds for seats in the theatre and the superintendent of the springs. For these they vote, and those who are appointed hold office from Panathenæa to Panathenæa. They vote also all the offices of the war department. And the Council is elected by lot to the number of five hundred, fifty from each tribe. And each of the tribes presides in turn as lot may assign, the first four thirty-six days each, and the six last thirty-five days each; for they reckon the year by the moon. The presidents first dine together in the Rotunda, at the expense of the state, then they assemble the Council and the people; the Council every day, unless there is a holiday, and the people four times during each presidency. They give public notice of all matters to be transacted by the Council, and what is to be taken each day, and what is not their business. They give public notice also of the meetings of the Assembly, one an ordinary one to confirm by vote magistrates if they are thought to discharge their duties efficiently, and to arrange about food and the protection of the country, and for such as want to prefer indictments to bring in such bills on this day, and to read out the registers of confiscations as well as the applications to the archon to be put in possession in cases of inheritance and of only daughters and heiresses, so that everybody may know if a case has gone by default. At the sixth presidency, in addition to what has just been stated, the opportunity is given of voting in cases of ostracism to confirm or otherwise, and of proceeding with the public prosecutions of common informers, both Athenians and resident-aliens up to three of each, where a promise has been made to the people and not performed. Another Assembly is assigned for supplications, so that anyone who wants may propose a supplication for anything he likes, either public or private, and discuss it with the people. The other two Assemblies attend to all other matters, and the laws ordain that at these meetings proposals should be considered to the number of three respectively regarding things sacred (or sacred moneys), heralds and embassies, and things profane (or public moneys). They sometimes deliberate even without any previous voting. The heralds and ambassadors come first before the presidents, and the bearers of letters deliver them into their hands.

CHAP. XLIV.: THE COUNCIL CONTINUED.

Now, there is one chief president, elected by lot; he holds office a day and a night, and it is not lawful for the same man to be appointed for a longer time, or to be appointed twice. He keeps the keys of the temples, in which are deposited the public moneys and records, as well as the state seal, and is obliged to remain in the Rotunda, as is also the third part of the presidents which he may order to do so. When the presidents summon the Council or people, he appoints by lot the nine chairmen (proedri), one from each tribe, except the tribe that presides, and from them again one as chief president, and he passes over to them the order of business. On receipt of it they preserve order, propose the matters to be deliberated on, decide the votings, and arrange things generally. They have power also to break up the meeting. It is not lawful to be chief president more than once in the year, while it is lawful to be a chairman (proedrus) once in each presidency. They elect boards of ten of generals and commanders of cavalry and of the other military officers of state in the Assembly, as the people may determine; these elections are made by the presidency after the sixth, when the omens are favourable, but a preliminary ordinance must be passed about these elections also.

CHAP. XLV.: DEPRIVED OF THE POWER OF PUTTING TO DEATH.

Now the Council formerly had power to punish by fines, to imprison, and to put to death. But on one occasion, as it was conducting Lysimachus to the executioner, who was awaiting him, Eukleides of Alopeke took him out of their hands, declaring that it was not right for any citizen to be put to death without the verdict of a court of law. On a trial being held in court, Lysimachus was acquitted, and got the surname of 'the man who escaped the cudgel.' Then the people deprived the Council of its power of putting to death and imprisoning and punishing by fines, and carried a law that in cases where the Council passed sentences or punished, the Thesmothetæ should bring the sentences and punishments before the court of justice, and that the vote of the jurors should be final. Now, the Council can try most of the officers of state, particularly such as have the management of money; but their decision is not final, and there is an appeal to the court of justice. Private individuals also have the right of indicting any officers of state they like for violating the laws, while such as are so indicted have also an appeal to the court of justice, if the Council finds them guilty. It examines also the members who are to compose the Council for the following year, and the nine archons. Formerly it had the power of rejection, but now in such cases there is an appeal to the court of justice. In the above matters then the Council does not possess final authority. Further, it submits preliminary ordinances to the people, and it is not lawful for the people to pass any measure which has not been thus submitted, or of which the presidents have not previously given public notice. For it is on these very grounds that the successful mover of a bill makes himself liable to an indictment for proposing unconstitutional measures.

CHAP. XLVI.: THE COUNCIL CONTINUED.

It superintends also the triremes, their equipment and their docks, and has new ships built, triremes or quadriremes, whichever the people votes, and equipment for them and docks. But the people votes designers for the vessels. And if they fail to hand over these quite complete to the new Council, they cannot get the present, for they get it during the following Council. It builds the triremes, choosing ten constructors out of the whole body. It examines also all public buildings, and if it decides that any wrong has been committed, it makes a presentment to the people against the offender, and if it finds him guilty, hands him over to a court of justice.

CHAP. XLVII.: THE TREASURERS OF ATHENA; THE GOVERNMENT-SELLERS.

It assists also in the management of all the remaining offices for the most part. For first there are the treasurers (of the temple) of Athena, ten in number, and appointed by lot, one from each tribe, from the Pentakosiomedimni according to Solon's law—for the law is still in force—and chief of them is he on whom the lot falls, however poor he may be. And they take over the image of Athena, and the victories, and all her other decorations, and the funds, in the presence of the Council. Then there are the government-sellers, ten in number, one being appointed by lot from each tribe. These farm out all the contracts and sell the productions of the mines, and, in conjunction with the military treasurer, and the presidents of funds for the payment of seats at the theatre, in the presence of the Council, ratify the farming of the taxes to him to whom the Council votes it; and they sell, in the presence of the Council, all the workable metals which are sold, both what have been sold for three years and what have been contracted for . . . and the property of those who have been banished by the Areopagus, and the archons confirm these transactions. They put up a public register on white tablets of the taxes that have been farmed out for a year . . . they pass over to the Council. They put up a public notice separately, in ten lists, of such as in each presidency have to make payments, and separately of such as have to do so at the end of the year, making a list for every payment, and separately of those in the ninth presidency. They give similar notice of the lands and houses which have been let and sold in the court of justice, for they also sell these . . . the sale price of houses must be paid for in five years, of land in ten. And they pay for these in the ninth presidency . . . and the king ratifies the lettings . . . and the letting of these also is for ten years, payment being made in the ninth presidency; for these reasons the largest amounts of money are collected in this presidency. Now the tablets on which the payments are recorded are brought to the Council, and the public notary keeps them. When payment is made he hands over to the receivers these very . . . But the rest is stored away separately. . . .

CHAP. XLVIII.: THE RECEIVERS; AUDITORS.

There are ten receivers appointed by lot by tribes. When they have received the lists, they cancel the moneys as they are paid in in the presence of the Council in the council-chamber, and again return the lists to the public notary. If anyone fails in payment the fact is then recorded, and the reason why; and he must pay the deficit or go to prison, and the Council has authority by law both to compel payment and to commit to prison. On the first day they receive the moneys and apportion them to the offices, and on the following they bring forward the apportionment, after recording it on a tablet, and draw up the list in the council-chamber, and . . . in the Council, if anyone, be he either magistrate or private individual, is known to have acted unfairly in the apportionment; and they put the question of his guilt to the vote. Further, the members of the Council appoint by lot from their own body tellers to the number of ten to account to the magistrates in each presidency. They appoint by lot also auditors, one from each tribe, and two assessors to each auditor, who are obliged to sit in the markets, which are called after those who have given their names to each tribe; and if anyone wishes at his own suit to prefer an audit against any of those who have given in their accounts within five days of their being given in, he writes on a white tablet his name and the name of the defendant, and the offences with which he charges him, and taking the valuation he decides upon, hands it over to the auditor. The auditor receives it, and if, after a hearing, he convicts, he hands over private cases to the jurors for the demes, which represent the particular tribe, while public cases he refers to the Thesmothetæ. The Thesmothetæ, if they entertain the suit, in their turn bring the audit before the court of justice, and the decision of the jurors is final.

CHAP. XLIX.: THE COUNCIL HOLDS A MUSTER OF THE KNIGHTS, ETC.

Further, the Council holds a muster of the horses, and if anyone having the means is found to keep his horse badly, it fines him in its keep; and to such as are unable to keep one, or unwilling to remain Knights, they bring up a wheel . . . . and he who is so treated is dishonoured. It holds also a muster of the cavalry scouts, to ascertain who appear to be fitted for such service, and the man against whom there is a show of hands is dismounted. It holds a muster also of the unmounted scouts, and if the show of hands is unfavourable, the man is no longer retained in the service. The registrars, whom the people appoints to the number of ten, make a list of the Knights. These pass over their names to the commanders of cavalry and the chiefs of the tribes, who take over the list and bring it to the Council. Then opening the tablet, in which the names of the Knights are signed and sealed, they cancel such of those as have been previously enrolled and solemnly swear that they are unable on physical grounds to serve as Knights; and they summon those who have been entered on the register, and whoever swears solemnly that he is unable to serve either on physical grounds or by reason of his means, they let him go; but the members of the Council decide by vote, in the case of any who does not so swear, whether he is fit to serve or not. If they decide that he is, they put him on the register, and if not, they let him also go. At one time the Council used to decide also about the plans for public buildings and the state-robe (peplos) of Athena, but now this is done by the court of justice on whom the lot falls; for the Council was thought to show favour in its decisions. It assists also in superintending the making of the victories and prizes for the Panathenæa in conjunction with the military treasurer. The Council examines also the disabled; for there is a law ordering it to examine such as are worth less than three minæ, and are physically so maimed as to be incapable of doing any work, and to give them from the public purse maintenance of two obols a day each; and a dispenser is appointed for them by lot. Further, it takes a part in the management of all the remaining offices, to speak generally. Such then are the various functions of the Council's administration.

CHAP. L: SURVEYORS OF TEMPLES; CITY MAGISTRATES.

Ten officers are appointed by lot to keep the temples in repair, and they expend the thirty minæ assigned by the receivers in repairing such as most require it. Ten city magistrates are similarly appointed, of whom five exercise their office in Peiræus and five in the city. Their duties are to see that the female flute-players and harpists and lute-players are not hired at more than two drachmæ, and if there is competition in the case of any of these employments they cast lots, and let it out to him on whom the lot falls. They make provision also against any dung-collector throwing down his dung near the wall, and prevent the building of houses in the highways, and the carrying of fences over the highways, and the constructing of waterpipes above ground with an outflow on the road, and making doors to open on the street. Lastly, they remove such as die on the highways, having public officers for this purpose.

CHAP. LI.: CLERKS OF THE MARKET; INSPECTORS OF WEIGHTS AND MEASURES, ETC.

Clerks of the market are also appointed by lot, five for Peiræus and five for the city. Their duty, as prescribed by law, is to see that commodities of all descriptions are sold pure and unadulterated. Appointed by lot also are the inspectors of weights and measures, five for the city and five for Peiræus; they look after measures and weights of all kinds, that sellers may use just ones. The corn-watchers appointed by lot used to be five for Peiræus and five for the city, but now there are twenty for the city and fifteen for Peiræus. They take measures to ensure, first, that the white (unprepared) corn in the market shall be offered for sale on fair terms, then that the millers shall sell their meal at prices based on the cost of the barley, and the bakers their bread at prices based on the cost of the wheat, and of the weight that they fix; for the law commands them to fix it. They appoint by lot ten superintendents of the market, and their duty is to superintend the markets, and of the corn that is imported into the corn-market to compel the merchants to bring two-thirds into the city.

CHAP. LII.: THE ELEVEN; SUITS DECIDED WITHIN A MONTH.

They appoint the Eleven also by lot to look after prisoners, and in the case of thieves and kidnappers and footpads who are committed to prison, if they confess, to punish them with death; but if they demand a trial, to bring them before the court of justice, and if they are acquitted to let them go, but if not, to put them to death at once; at the same time they have to produce before the court the inventories of the lands and houses of criminals, and to deliver over to the government-sellers what is decided to be confiscated, and to prefer the indictments; for this last is the duty of the Eleven, except that in some cases it devolves on the Thesmothetæ. They

41

appoint by lot also five officers, one for two tribes, to receive informations, and bring into court the cases which have to be decided within a month of their commencement. These suits are heard without fees in the case of a debtor not paying, and of a person borrowing at twelve per cent. and defrauding, and of anyone in the marketplace wishing to work and borrowing from anybody on a pretext, and, further, in cases of assault, subscriptions, dealings, slaves, cattle, the fitting out of a trireme for the public service, and banking. Now they institute and adjudicate on such suits within the month, and the receivers act similarly both on behalf of and against the farmers of the taxes, having power to adjudicate in cases up to ten drachmæ, but taking all others which have to be decided within the month into court.

CHAP. LIII.: JUDICIAL OFFICERS; ARBITRATORS.

They appoint by lot also forty, four from each tribe, before whom parties bring all other suits. Their number was formerly thirty, and they used to administer justice by going on circuit throughout the demes, but after the oligarchy of the Thirty they were increased to forty. Cases up to ten drachmæ they have full power to decide, but such as are above this amount they pass over to the arbitrators. These take them over, and if they are unable to effect a settlement, state their opinions, and if both sides are satisfied with their recommendations and abide by them, the suit is at an end. But if one of the parties appeals to the court, they put the evidence and challenges and laws into vases, using a separate vase both for the plaintiff and the defendant, and signing and sealing them, with the judgment of the arbitrator recorded on a tablet attached, they hand them over to the adjudicators of the tribe to which the defendant belongs. These adjudicators take them over and bring them into the court, which is composed of two hundred and one for amounts within a thousand drachmæ, and of four hundred and one for amounts above a thousand. They are not allowed to make use of any laws or challenges or evidence other than what is received from the arbitrator and contained in the vases. Arbitrators must be sixty years of age; and this is evident from the archons and Eponymi. For there are ten Eponymi *Endnote 015* of the tribes and forty-two of the ages, and the Ephebi in former days at the time of their enrolment had their names registered on white tablets, and the name of the archon in whose time they were enrolled was added to the register as well as that of the Eponymus who had acted as arbitrator in the previous year; but now their names are inscribed on a brass pillar, and the pillar stands before the council-chamber near the statues of the ten Eponymi of the tribes. And the forty, taking the last one of the Eponymi, assign the arbitrations to them, and by lot in what cases each shall act. For the law ordains forfeiture of political rights in the case of anyone of the proper age failing to act as arbitrator, unless he happens to be filling any other office, or to be abroad; in such cases only is exemption granted. Anyone who has been wronged by an arbitrator is free to indict him before the jurors, but if their verdict goes against him he loses his political rights, as the laws ordain; but even then there is the right of appeal. They make use also of the names of the Eponymi with regard to military expeditions, and when they send out a body of young men, they publicly notify from and up to what archon and Eponymus they are to serve.

CHAP. LIV.: SURVEYORS OF ROADS; AUDITORS; SECRETARIES.

They appoint also by lot the following officers: Five surveyors of roads, who have public workmen assigned to them, and whose duty it is to keep the roads in repair; and ten auditors with ten advocates to assist them. To these last all office-holders are bound to submit their accounts, for they alone check the accounts of such as are responsible, and lay their audits before the court. If they convict anyone of theft, the jurors find him guilty of theft, and he is fined ten times the amount of what has been detected; and if they convict anyone of taking bribes, and the jurors find him guilty, they condemn him in the amount of the bribes, and in addition he has to pay a fine of ten times that amount; and if they find him guilty of a wrong they condemn him in the amount of the wrong, and he is fined this amount simply if it is paid before the ninth presidency: if not, it is doubled; but the tenfold fine is not doubled. They appoint also by lot an officer who is called the secretary for the presidency, and is at the head of the secretaries, and keeps the decrees that are passed, and makes minutes of all proceedings, and sits by the Council. Now, in former times he was elected by vote, and men of the highest distinction and character used to be appointed to the office; for his name is inscribed on pillars, attached to treaties of alliance and friendship with foreigners, and public measures (or, citizenships); but now the election is made by lot. They appoint by lot also a second secretary for the laws, who sits by the Council, and he also makes a copy of all of them. The people also by vote elects a secretary to read out documents to itself and the Council, and his authority does not extend further. It appoints also by lot ten superintendents of sacred rites, who have the designation of 'for the sacrifices,' and perform the sacrifices appointed by oracle, and when there is occasion to obtain good omens, obtain them in conjunction with the diviners. It appoints by lot also ten others, who are designated by the year, and perform certain sacrifices; they superintend all the festivals celebrated at intervals of five years, with the single exception of the

Panathenæa, as follows: one at Delos (where it is celebrated also every seven years), the second the Brauronia, the third the Heraklea, and the fourth the Panathenæa at Eleusis; and none of them occurs in the same year. . . . . They appoint by lot also a governor for Salamis and a demarch for Peiræus, who hold the Dionysia in both places and appoint Choregi (to defray the expenses of bringing out a chorus).

CHAP. LV.: THE ARCHONS; HOW THEY ARE APPOINTED.

These then are the officers appointed by lot, and their powers in their several departments are as has been just described. Now as to those who have the title of the nine archons, an account has been already given of how they were appointed at first. But now they appoint by lot six Thesmothetæ and a secretary for them, and further, an archon and king and commander-in-chief severally from each tribe. And they are first examined in the Council by the five hundred, except the secretary, who is examined only in the court just like all other officers of state (for all who are appointed either by lot or vote hold office only after examination), but the nine archons are examined before the Council and again in court. In former days no one could hold office if he were rejected by the Council, but now there is appeal to the court, and with it rests the decision regarding the examination. The questions asked in the examination are as follows: First, who is your father, and of what deme? and who your father's father, and who your mother, and who your mother's father, and of what deme? and, after this, if Apollo is his family and Zeus his household god, and where their temples are; then, if they have tombs, and where they are; and, last, if he treats his parents well, and pays his taxes, and has duly performed his military service. Having asked these questions, the examiner says, 'Call your witnesses to these facts.' When the witnesses are produced he asks further, 'Has anyone any accusation to bring against this man?' and if no one comes forward, after giving opportunity for accusation and defence, he proposes the show of hands in the Council and in the court the vote. And if no one wants to accuse, he at once gives his vote. Formerly one only put his pebble into the urn, but now all must do so. Further, the right exists of passing a vote about them with the object, if any bad man gets his accusers out of the way, of putting it in the power of the jurors to reject him. When the examination has been concluded in this way, they walk up to the stone underneath which are the treasuries, and on which the arbitrators take their oath and declare their awards, and witnesses solemnly swear to their evidence. Mounting this stone, they swear that they will discharge the duties of their office faithfully and according to the laws, and that they will not take bribes in connection with their office, and if they should they will make a votive offering of a gold statue. After this oath they walk to the Acropolis, and take it again in the same terms there, and after this they enter upon their office.

CHAP. LVI.: THE ARCHON (EPONYMUS); HIS DUTIES.

The archon and king and commander-in-chief take assessors, two each, whomever they like; these are examined in the court before they can act, and after appointment are responsible for their official conduct. The archon, as soon as ever he enters on office, first makes proclamation that, whatever a man possessed before he entered on office, that he shall possess and be master of to the end of his term of office. Then he provides Choregi for the tragic poets, the three richest men of all the Athenians. Formerly he used also to provide five for the comic poets, but for them the tribes now contribute. After receiving the Choregi brought by the tribes for the Dionysia for men and boys and comic actors, and for the Thargelia for men and boys (those for the Dionysia being furnished by tribes, and for the Thargelia, one for two tribes, each of the two tribes contributing its quota for these), he makes the challenges and brings forward the excuses. . . . For the Choregus who furnishes boys must be more than forty years of age. He appoints also for Delos Choregi, and the chief priest for the vessel with thirty benches that takes the young men. And he used to superintend the processions of the festival in honour of Asklepius, when the initiated keep within doors, and of the great Dionysia, in conjunction with its superintendents, whom in former days the people used to vote to the number of ten, and they used to defray out of their own pockets the expenses of the procession; but now it appoints by lot one from each tribe, and gives a hundred minæ to the preparations for it. He superintends also the procession in the Thargelia and that in honour of Zeus the Saviour. He too manages the games of the Dionysia, as well as of the Thargelia. Leave to make public indictments and bring private actions is obtained from him, and after holding a preliminary inquiry, he brings them into court as follows: ill-treatment of the young (in which anyone can prosecute who likes, without incurring any penalty), ill-treatment of orphans (these are against their guardians), ill-treatment of an heir (these are against his guardian and those whom he lives with), damage to a house belonging to an orphan (these are also against the guardians), mental derangement (when anyone accuses another of ruining himself by reason of mental derangement), the appointment of distributers when anyone refuses to divide property that is held in common, appointment of guardians, settlement of disputed claims of guardianship, if several wish to make a man

45

guardian of the same female ward, and settlement of disputed claims in cases of inheritances and only daughters and heiresses. He superintends also the charge of orphans and heirs, and of all such women as on the death of their husbands claim to be pregnant. He has power also to punish wrong-doers, or to bring them before the court. He lets also the houses of orphans and heirs . . . and becomes distributer and receives the mortgages . . . gives the children the food which he gets in. So he superintends all these matters.

CHAP. LVII.: THE KING ARCHON; HIS DUTIES.

The king, in the first place, has the management of the mysteries in conjunction with the superintendents whom the people elect, two in number, out of the whole body of Athenians, one from the Eumolpidæ and one from the Heralds; and secondly of the Lenæan Dionysia . . . this procession then the king and the superintendents conduct in common; but the king arranges the games. He arranges also all the torchraces. And it is he, so to say, who manages all the ancient sacrifices. Leave to bring actions for profaneness is obtained from him, and in the case of any dispute about priesthood he awards the penalty. It is he who adjudicates all disputes about honours between families and priests. From him leave is obtained to bring the action in all cases of murder, and it is he who proclaims interdiction from customary rights. Now, there are actions both for murder and wounding. In murder of malice prepense, the case is tried in the Areopagus, and so with poisoning and arson; for the only cases that the Council tries are homicide, unintentional or intentional, if the person killed is a servant, either a resident-alien or foreigner, and the trial is then held in the Palladium. If a person admits an act of homicide, but justifies it as legal, as catching an adulterer, or in war from not knowing who he was, or when competing in a contest, they hold the trial in the Palladium. If a person has to remain in exile on a charge of murder or wounding, under circumstances in which the relatives may relent, the trial is held in the Phreatto; and he makes his defence in a boat moored off the shore, and commissioners appointed by lot conduct the trial, except in cases that come before the Areopagus: and the king introduces the suit and they try it . . . and in the open air. And the king, when he tries the case, takes off his crown. The accused for the rest of the time is not allowed to take part in religious services, and no one can bring the charge against him; then entering the temple he makes his defence; and when anyone declares who has committed the act, he obtains leave to bring an action against him. And the king and the tribe-kings try all cases concerning things without life, as well as all animals.

CHAP. LVIII: THE COMMANDER-IN-CHIEF, POLEMARCH

The commander-in-chief makes sacrifices in the feast of Artemis the huntress and Enualios, and arranges the funeral games held in honour of such as have been killed in war. Leave is obtained from him to bring such private suits as may arise with the resident-aliens, those who pay alike (a favoured class of resident-aliens), and the friends of the state. It is his duty to take and divide ten parts, and apportion to each tribe the part that falls to its lot, and assign the judges of the tribe to the arbitrators. And he himself brings into court the actions against freedmen for default to their patrons, and against resident-aliens for not choosing a patron, and cases of inheritance and only daughters and heiresses for the resident-aliens, and in all matters generally the commander-in-chief acts for the resident-aliens in the same way as the archon does for the citizens.

CHAP. LIX.: THE THESMOTHETÆ; THEIR FUNCTIONS.

To the Thesmothetæ belongs first the right of publicly notifying on what days the courts of law are to sit, and then of assigning them to the magistrates; for as they assign, the magistrates must use them. Further, they bring before the people all bills of indictment and condemnations by show of hands, and votes directing public prosecutions, and indictments for proposing unconstitutional measures and bad laws, and the audits of the chairmen (proedri) and chief president of the Council, and of the generals. And public indictments are brought before them in which small money deposits are made, viz., in the case of an alien for usurping civic rights, and for bribing the judges to declare him a citizen, and of having obtained acquittal in such actions by means of bribery, and of false accusation, and bribes, and false-registering, and false citation, and intention to kill, and state-debtors for getting their names cancelled before payment, and adultery. They introduce also the examinations for all offices of state, and the rejected candidates for membership in the deme, and condemnations by the Council. They introduce also private suits, concerned with trade, mines, and slaves for slandering a freeman. They assign by lot to the magistrates all their courts, both public and private. They ratify the judicial agreements with the subject cities, and bring in the suits arising from them, as well as false evidence in the Areopagus. And the nine archons, together with the secretary of the Thesmothetæ, appoint by lot all the jurors, each those of his own tribe. Such then are the duties of the nine archons.

CHAP. LX.: THE DIRECTORS OF GAMES; THE SACRED OIL.

They appoint also by lot ten directors of games, one for each tribe. They, after approval, hold office for four years, and manage the procession of the Panathenæa, the musical and gymnastic contests and the horse-races, and, in conjunction with the Council, have Athena's state-robe and the vases made, and apportion to the successful competitors the oil which is made from the sacred olives. And the archon levies the tax from the owners of the grounds in which the sacred olives grow, a kotyle and a half (i.e., about three-quarters of a pint) for each stem, whereas in former times the state used to sell the produce, and if anyone dug up or broke a sacred olive-tree, the council of Areopagus used to try, and if it found him guilty, punish him with death. Since the owner of the land has contributed the oil, the law indeed has continued in force, but the trial has become a dead-letter, while the oil from the cuttings, but not from the stems, still belongs to the state. The archon then, having collected what accrues during his tenure of office, hands it over to the treasurers in the Acropolis, and is not allowed to go up to the Acropolis before he has handed over the whole of it to the treasurers. The treasurers then keep it in the Acropolis till the celebration of the Panathenæa, when they measure it out to the directors of games, and they again to the victorious competitors. Now for the victors in the musical contests the prizes are of silver and gold, in those for manliness spears, and for the gymnastic games and horse-races olive-oil.

CHAP. LXI.: ELECTION BY VOTE TO ALL OFFICES OF WAR DEPARTMENT.

They elect by vote also to all offices, without exception, connected with the war department, the generals in former times being elected one from each tribe, but now from all. They assign them their duties by vote, appointing one to the command of the hoplites, who leads the members of his deme if they go on foreign service; one in command of the country which he protects, and who, if war breaks out in it, takes part in the war; two in command of Peiræus, the one for Munychia, the other for the shore, who have charge of Phyle and matters in the Peiræus; and one to the command of the symmoriæ (companies, consisting of sixty members each, of the twelve hundred wealthiest citizens), who makes out the list of those who have to fit out a trireme for the public service, and allows them challenges, and brings into court their cases for adjudication; the rest they commission according to circumstances. A vote is passed in each presidency as to their conduct in office; if it is adverse, the trial is held in court, and in case of conviction a proper punishment or fine is awarded; while in case of acquittal, the accused continues in office for the remainder of his term. They have the power when on service of placing under arrest anyone not conforming to discipline, and publicly proclaiming his name, and inflicting a fine; to the last however they rarely resort. They appoint also by vote ten commanders of divisions, one for each tribe, and he commands his tribesmen and appoints captains, and further two commanders of cavalry out of the whole body of citizens. These take command of the knights, five tribes being assigned to each, and are invested with the same powers as the generals possess in the case of the hoplites, while in their case also a vote is passed on their conduct. They appoint by lot also chiefs of tribes, one for the tribe, to command the knights in the same way as commanders of divisions do the hoplites. They vote also a commander of cavalry for Lemnos to superintend the knights there, and a treasurer for the sacred trireme Paralus, and another for that of Ammon.

CHAP. LXII.: PAY ATTACHED TO OFFICES

Now the officers of state appointed by lot were in former times those so appointed, together with the nine archons, from the whole tribe, and the election of the officers now appointed in the Theseum was distributed among the demes; but since the demes used to sell these offices, they have elected to them also by lot from the whole tribe, except the members of the Council and the guards, which they now assign to the members of the demes. They receive pay first for all other assemblies a drachma, but for the ordinary assembly a drachma and a half; then in the courts three obols; then the Council five obols . . . . again, the nine archons receive for maintenance four obols each, and maintain besides a herald and a flute-player, while the governor of Salamis receives a drachma a day. The directors of games dine in the Prytaneum during the month of Hecatombæon, *Endnote 016* in which the Panathenæa are celebrated, beginning on the fourth of the month. The Amphictyones who are sent to Delos receive a drachma a day during the time they are there; and the magistrates who are commissioned to Samos, Scyros, Lemnos or Imbros receive in every case money for their maintenance. It is allowable to hold military offices several times, but not a single other one, except that you may be twice a member of the Council.

CHAP. LXIII.: APPOINTMENT OF JURORS.

The nine archons elect by lot the jurors for the courts by tribes, while the secretary to the Thesmothetæ is elected from the tenth tribe. The entrances into the courts are ten, one for each tribe; the balloting-urns twenty, two for each tribe; and the boxes a hundred, ten for each tribe;

there are ten other boxes besides, in which are cast the tablets of the jurors on whom the lot falls. And two balloting - urns and staves are placed at each entrance for each juror, and tickets are put in the urn to the number of the staves, and on them are written the letters of the alphabet, beginning from the eleventh (l), corresponding in number to the courts that are to be supplied with jurors. Anyone may serve above thirty years of age, who is not a debtor to the state and has not suffered deprivation of political rights; but if anyone serves who has not the right to do so he is indicted in the court, and if found guilty, the jurors inflict upon him such punishment or penalty as he seems to deserve. If he is fined, he must remain in prison till he has paid the former debt on account of which he was indicted, and any additional fine that the court may impose. Each juror has a tablet made of boxwood, on which is inscribed his own name, with his father's and his deme, and one of the letters of the alphabet up to k; for the jurors are distributed by tribes into ten groups, and are about equal in number for each letter. After the Thesmothetes has allotted the additional letters to be assigned to the jurors, the attendant brings and puts up on each court the letter which has been drawn.

ENDNOTES:

Endnote 002

Thesmothetes. As this word means 'law-giver,' 'legislator,' it seems better, to prevent misapprehension, to retain it in its Greek form. This passage tells us why they were originally appointed; frequent references are made to them elsewhere in the book, and their duties will be found detailed in chap. lix.

Endnote 003

The medimnus=about 1½ bushel.

Endnote 004

These were of a triangular pyramidical form, written on the three sides and turned round on a pivot.

Endnote 005

Government-sellers. Their duties are described in chap. xlvii., and those of 'the Eleven' in chap. lii. The Kolakratæ in old times had the general charge of the finances.

Endnote 006

No doubt a return of the aristocratic government.

Endnote 007

Literally, at Pallenis, i.e., the temple of Pallenis Athena, Herodotus, i., 62; Pallene being a deme of Attica, where Athena had a temple.

Endnote 008

Families, i.e., collections of families, 'clans,' 'houses.'

Endnote 009

Or, they had no names of their own; these are the alternative renderings, as suggested by the British Museum editor.

Endnote 010

Compare Herodotus, i. 165, telling how the Phocæans, on deserting their native city, sunk iron in the sea, and swore never to return till it came up again to the surface.

Endnote 011

Trustees of the Greeks, appointed by Athens to levy the contributions paid by the Greek states towards the Persian war.

Especially as commanders of cavalry.

This month corresponds to from the middle of May to the middle of June; Skirophorion, a few lines further on, is the following month.

He being the archon who gave his name to the year (Eponymus).

Eponymi—i.e., giving their names to the tribes and the forty-two ages, viz., from eighteen to sixty, the period of military service.

This month extended from the middle of July to the middle of August.

Made in the USA
Columbia, SC
30 September 2018